A Parallel Between The Two Trials of Lord George Sackville, Lately Published. Pointing Out Their Difference: With Occasional Remarks. In Which The Evidence and Matter are Compared and Canvassed, and a Light Thrown Upon The Whole Process

Anonymous

A Parallel Between The Two Trials of Lord George Sackville, Lately Published. Pointing Out Their Difference: With Occasional Remarks. In Which The Evidence and Matter are Compared and Canvassed, and a Light Thrown Upon The Whole Process
A Parallel between the Two Trials of Lord George Sackville - 1760
HAR03993
Monograph
Harvard Law School Library
London: Printed for J. Pridden at The Feathers in Fleet-Street, Near Fleet-Bridge, 1760

The Making of Modern Law collection of legal archives constitutes a genuine revolution in historical legal research because it opens up a wealth of rare and previously inaccessible sources in legal, constitutional, administrative, political, cultural, intellectual, and social history. This unique collection consists of three extensive archives that provide insight into more than 300 years of American and British history. These collections include:

Legal Treatises, 1800-1926: over 20,000 legal treatises provide a comprehensive collection in legal history, business and economics, politics and government.

Trials, 1600-1926: nearly 10,000 titles reveal the drama of famous, infamous, and obscure courtroom cases in America and the British Empire across three centuries.

Primary Sources, 1620-1926: includes reports, statutes and regulations in American history, including early state codes, municipal ordinances, constitutional conventions and compilations, and law dictionaries.

These archives provide a unique research tool for tracking the development of our modern legal system and how it has affected our culture, government, business – nearly every aspect of our everyday life. For the first time, these high-quality digital scans of original works are available via print-on-demand, making them readily accessible to libraries, students, independent scholars, and readers of all ages.

The BiblioLife Network

This project was made possible in part by the BiblioLife Network (BLN), a project aimed at addressing some of the huge challenges facing book preservationists around the world. The BLN includes libraries, library networks, archives, subject matter experts, online communities and library service providers. We believe every book ever published should be available as a high-quality print reproduction; printed on-demand anywhere in the world. This insures the ongoing accessibility of the content and helps generate sustainable revenue for the libraries and organizations that work to preserve these important materials.

The following book is in the "public domain" and represents an authentic reproduction of the text as printed by the original publisher. While we have attempted to accurately maintain the integrity of the original work, there are sometimes problems with the original work or the micro-film from which the books were digitized. This can result in minor errors in reproduction. Possible imperfections include missing and blurred pages, poor pictures, markings and other reproduction issues beyond our control. Because this work is culturally important, we have made it available as part of our commitment to protecting, preserving, and promoting the world's literature.

GUIDE TO FOLD-OUTS MAPS and OVERSIZED IMAGES

The book you are reading was digitized from microfilm captured over the past thirty to forty years. Years after the creation of the original microfilm, the book was converted to digital files and made available in an online database.

In an online database, page images do not need to conform to the size restrictions found in a printed book. When converting these images back into a printed bound book, the page sizes are standardized in ways that maintain the detail of the original. For large images, such as fold-out maps, the original page image is split into two or more pages

Guidelines used to determine how to split the page image follows:

- Some images are split vertically; large images require vertical and horizontal splits.
- For horizontal splits, the content is split left to right.
- For vertical splits, the content is split from top to bottom.
- For both vertical and horizontal splits, the image is processed from top left to bottom right.

A PARALLEL

BETWEEN THE

TWO TRIALS,

OF

Lord GEORGE SACKVILLE,

Lately publifhed

Pointing out their Difference:

With Occafional

REMARKS.

IN WHICH

The Evidence and Matter are compared and canvaffed, and a Light thrown upon the Whole PROCESS.

LONDON

Printed for J PRIDDEN at the Feathers in Fleet-Street, near Fleet-Bridge, 1760

Rec June 20, 1904

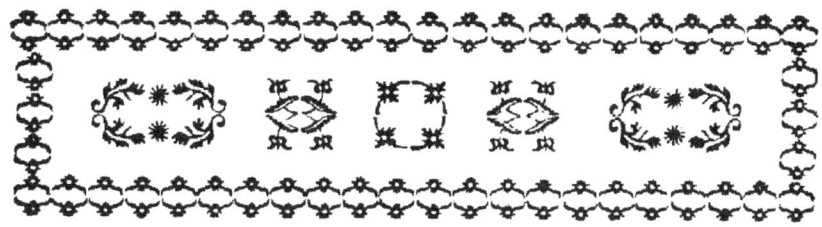

A

PARALLEL, &c.

IN consequence of Lord George Sackville's follicitations for a trial, he obtained one, and now it is over, there have been two copies of the proceedings published. The design of these pages is to point out the differences. And we shall begin with stating some hints concerning their publication.

If we may credit the tongue of public report, that entitled "The Trial of Lord "George Sackville, *printed for W. Owen*," is done at the request or direction of Mr. S-------e or his friends. But that entitled, "The proceedings of a court martial, *print-* "*ed for A. Millar*," is printed by the order of the Judge Advocate, and consequently looked upon as the most authentic and correct, while the other, on the first information, carries with it an air of partiality, but how far it is true, the following pages will determine.

A parallel drawn between the two printed trials, seems the best channel through which to steer towards truth, and to avoid even the shadow of bias, or prejudice, this seems the more requisite, in an age so perplexed with divisions, and so embarassed with chicanery, that without minuteness and precision, some things would prove inexplicable to readers, and others not to be accounted for; in order to frame this parallel, we have, by adhering closely to each particular, page by page, by looking at every side of the object attentively, and with candor, endeavoured to make a developement of the whole, so that the reader will find this not only to be a parallel, by which from filtrating, and ventilating the particulars, the truth of the matter may be come at, but also, on perusal he will find it an extract, or short detail of facts, by which he will avoid the prolixity of a long process, wherein repetition cannot be avoided. Having premised thus much, we proceed to the trials before us, which we shall distinguish by, first, Lord George's trial. Secondly, the Judge advocate's Account.

First, Lord George's trial begins with an objection, seconded by reasons, against the sitting of General Belford in the Court-Martial, he thought him prejudiced, as there

there did some time since subsist a difference between them, which he found did not cease, from observing that General Belford was the only field officer of his acquaintance, that did not visit him on his return from England; his Lordship is very delicate and tender, notwithstanding, of the General's honour, but pleads the natural tendency in men's minds to be imperceptibly biassed, for making this objection. General Belford answers that he did not come to sit there, as may appear by the impropriety of his dress, but says nothing as to the neglect in not visiting. This distinction is not observed in the Judge Advocate's account, beside that, General Belford is set down as a sitting member of the court on the first day of Lord George Sackville's trial, and not in the Advocate's, which shews that he came with an intent to sit, though not suitably dressed, but on his insisting to be excused, Major General Julius Cæsar sat in his place.

The Judge Advocate, on the first day, Feb. 29. by Lord George's trial, page 8th. says, that he is directed to confine the charge to such orders as he received relative *to the battle of Minden*.

Lord George excepts against this expression, as too general, and says, *To the day of the battle*. Judge Advocate replies, *relative to it*. Lord George rejoins, *relative to it,* it, *tho' preceding it,* which the Judge Advocate acquiesces in. This is the only distinction to be observed on the first day, wherein General Onslow sat as president, but on his illness, Lieutenant General Howard supplied his place.

Second day, Friday March 7

The commission of Lord George and the King's instructions read and admitted by Lord George (page 9th of Lord George's trial) the Judge Advocate says to Col Johnston, the witness, Lord George Sackville stands here, charged with DISOBEDIENCE OF ORDERS, did you make any observations relative to that; Lord George objects, *Sir, if we are to go into hearsay, and opinion, you may sit here some months Colonel Legonier attends on the part of the crown, what passed between him and me, I dare say he will declare upon oath.* General Cholmondely also remarks upon this, in Lord George's trial, page 9, *He has told you,* (viz. the Judge Advocate) *that Colonel Legonier told him that he had carried orders for Lord George Sackville to come up with the cavalry, so that here is hearsay evidence already.* No notice taken of this evidence in the Judge Advocate's account.

On Captain Winchingrode's evidence (according to Lord George's trial, p. 9) that evidence being a foreigner, and having an
inter-

interpreter, it is previously desired by Lord George that the oath be explained to him, with the methods of the laws of England, in regard to testimony in Courts of Justice, after which the Judge Advocate tells him, that the penalties in cases of perjury are very severe, the Court may punish at discretion, or adjudge it transportation for seven years. This circumstance is omitted in the Judge Advocate's account.

Remark.

Perhaps it was thought immaterial, probably it was so, but it should seem that Lord George did not think it so, as the evidence was first, a foreigner,, secondly, aid de camp to Prince Ferdinand, and therefore likely to be influenced; and lastly, because he was the person who brought the express orders from Prince Ferdinand, to Lord George, three very material reasons why he should be solemnly reminded of the importance and consequence of the oath administered, and the consequence which was to attend the truth, or falsehood of it, for being a creature and dependent on Prince Ferdinand, a favourable evidence on the side of Lord George, must cast a reflection on his commander

It seems (from Lord George's trial page 25) that his Lordship was willing to go through with the examination of Colonel Fitzroy, for General Cholmondely, says,---*My Lord George Sackville, you will not have time to go through the examination of Colonel Fitzroy now,---you may go through it at once,* to which Lord George says, *I had much rather not be interrupted in my examination if the Court pleases, I would chuse to finish without interruption.* Not mentioned in the Judge Advocate's account.

Fourth Day.

(In Lord George's trial page 28) Lord George in the course of his examining Colonel Fitzroy, asks him, *Did you see Captain Smith sent back by me towards the cavalry, as soon as it had passed the wood,* to which Colonel Fitzroy answers, *he did.* Lord George then asks, *did you know his orders,* Colonel Fitzroy answers, *I did not, I have already mentioned that I did not hear them distinct enough.* Lord George subjoins, *you did mention that you did not hear the conversation, you might hear the orders, though not the conversation,* to which distinction Colonel Fitzroy says, *I did not.* This is omitted in the Judge Advocate's account, it seems nevertheless to Lord George a material distinction, as if Colonel Fitzroy was somewhat reserved in telling all he knew, intimating plainly that he must have heard the orders

orders given, though he might not be master of the whole conversation.

(In Lord George's trial page 29.) Lord George asks Colonel Fitzroy *if the wood was equally thick, as well as equally open through which the cavalry was to pass,* Colonel Fitzroy answers, *that it was equally open, when he went through it*, and adds, *I must observe that no part of the line was engaged when I came away*, this omitted in the Judge Advocate's account, upon which observation of Colonel Fitzroy, Lord George says, *then my former question must be varied*, and asks then, what distance there was between the lines that were forming, and that part of the lines, that was advancing, to which variation in the question Colonel Fitzroy answers, *I make the same answer, I think some distance, not very great.*

OBSERVATION.

Lord George, had before asked, (Lord Sackville's trial page 28) what distance was there between the second line of infantry, and the enemy's infantry engaged with the British infantry? to which (previous to the varied question) Colonel Fitzroy, had answered,---I don't know, as that distance varied almost every instant. There were two lines of the British infantry engaged, a brigade of the second engaged when the first engaged. There was no part of the first or second line engaged when I came away, here the Colonel seems to vary in his evidence, as to precision, in this answer, he says, that no part of *the second or first line engaged*, when he came away; in the subsequent answer, which caused Lord George to vary the question, he says, that no *part of the line* was engaged.

The words, no *part of the line*, and no part of the second or first line were engaged, differ materially, and essentially, hereupon General Cholmondely, (page 29, Lord George's trial) observes with reluctance, and says, --- *I am sorry that the Court goes on, without a more particular examination into facts, by the members. The Judge Advocate asks questions very proper*, but the transactions of that day he is *not* a judge of, *I must therefore, ask some questions necessary for the information of the Court, I do it with the utmost reluctance, and I mention this, that the odium if any may not lie upon me*

In Lord Sackville's trial, and omitted in the Judge Advocate's (page 31) the Court asks, was there any cavalry in the rear of our infantry to have supported them, to which Colonel Fitzroy answers, there was none. The Court, (perhaps General Cholmondely, who seems in possession of the Question) says, --- *Then are you of opinion, that if they had been broke, the whole must have*

have been facrificed. Lord George, interrupts here, and says,---*Sir, I don't think that a fair queftion, to afk only matter of opinion,* and the Prefident anfwers,---*if you defire it, we will clear the Court to debate it,* to which Lord George, replies.---" Sir, I did not mention it as an objection to clear the Court, or to prevent the truth coming out; I would not have defired a trial if that had been the cafe I never yet heard, it could be faid, I was brought here by any other defire than my own; therefore if I object to this, or to any thing that tended to go to the bottom of the affair, I fhould think I deferved the worft of punifhments, the reafon I mentioned it was, for the dignity of the Court, and for the fake of the method of proceeding in Court-Martials; that the Generals who fit here, fhould afk the opinion of fo young a Gentleman, as Colonel Fitzroy: The witneffes are to lay down facts for your information, and the judgment of the generals, is to decide upon them Every officer is able to determine upon this queftion, *viz.* If the infantry is broke upon a plain, and cavalry near at hand, to fuftain them, there is no doubt but it would be of great fervice, fuch queftions of opinion cannot be for the information of the court, but for the audience; I am tried for difobedience of orders. the queftion is, did I difobey the orders of

Prince

Prince Ferdinand? but whether the cavalry did or did not attack is not a charge upon me, but upon those who gave me the orders; when I have said this, I hope I shall be equally allowed the liberty of putting questions to the witnesses, as to matters of opinion. The only reason, that induced me to mention it was, that the dignity of the Court may not be so let down, as to form their determinations upon the opinion of Colonel Fitzroy."

REMARK.

It will not be denied, by the most prejudiced on either side, but the not admitting the opinion of a young officer, consulted by old experienced Generals, was seasonably urged by the Defendant, beside to ask what would be the issue of such or such a motion, seems foreign to the question in hand, whether Lord George had obeyed Prince Ferdinand's orders, to ask questions and opinions upon suppositious circumstances, events that may not, and in this case, did not happen, seems no way relative to the points or demerits of the cause in hand.

(In page 40, Lord George's trial) upon Colonel Sloper's evidence falling very hard upon Lord George (a circumstance omitted in the Judge Advocate's account) Lord George speaks to the President thus, " Sir, Charles

Charles Howard, if I may be allowed to say a word, touching this gentleman's evidence before I go any further, and General Cholmondely's agreeing to indulge the Prisoner, Lord George complains of it in the following manner. It is hard for me to sit here, and have a witness come against me, with an opinion of this nature, while I am forced to remain entirely silent; I shall only say a few words. This sort of attack I never heard of before, from any one Gentleman whatever, excepting from the private insinuations of this gentleman, now before the Court, I heard of it since he has been in London, I am glad that he has mentioned it in Court, I"------Interrupted by Lord Albermarle, who says, " Your Lordship will have an opportunity of observing upon that in your defence, but I am afraid, we are going into an irregularity." To which Lord Geore replies, with some warmth, " I will only say now, that I shall prove my conduct that day, with regard to every branch of it, and I shall shew that Gentleman, to the Court in such colours for truth, and veracity."-- Interrupted again by Lord Albermarle. " My Lord this is being irregular. Lord George answers, Your Lordship may imagine what I must feel on this occasion, and it is difficult not to express it instantly. Lord Albermarle, tells him to this, " I am sensible what your Lordship
must

must feel, and am sorry to interrupt---but for the sake of proceeding," to which Lord George says, " I submit to the opinion of the court, and must beg leave to suppose, for the present, that no such evidence has been given; I shall now go on, as if nothing of this sort had happened, and shall treat that gentleman in that part of his evidence with all the contempt it deserves."

OBSERVATION.

Lord George, in his defence, and speaking to the evidence given in by Colonel Sloper, charges him with having been profuse of his invectives to all people and in all places, both in Germany and in London; and that as he knew he had told his tale to so many people, and in so many places, he was afraid and ashamed to deny upon oath, what he had averred and repeated so often: It may be doubted whether private observations, private discourses, or opinions, should be admitted in cases of life and death; less so, where reputation was concerned; for how can any man, who is an evidence, be permitted to leave matter of fact for digressions, or judge of the internal disposition of the mind by the external appearance, where hurry in reflection on the present operation may dissipate the spirits, and cause a visible confusion fufion in the countenance, which might be interpreted as fear and corwadice, efpecially by the eye of prejudice----the words, *that man,* fpeaking of Lord George, who, in his military capacity, as fuperior in command, might have exacted more refpect from an inferior officer, feem to bear the face of contempt, and muft, in fome meafure, tend to influence the judgment of the unbiaffed, in disfavour of any evidence that may fubfequently come after. If it was his opinion, that Lord George was actuated from the motives of pannick, he was not obliged on the face of his evidence to fay fo; but we find him officious to tell private difcourfe, which no body required him to publifh; nay, he appears to be affiduous to know if he may have leave. We beg leave in this parallel to advance fo much, fince an appeal to the publick, is the laft of all appeals; nor could we call this a Parallel with Remarks, &c. if we were averfe from judging by that criterion, which muft in the end, determine every procedure of this nature, to obtrude a private opinion on a fet of refpectable judges, to ftigmatize an unhappy man in the crime, when he ftands to vindicate his conduct, is like knocking a man's brains out, when he is attempting to fwim for life to the fhore. In cafes of life and death, the judge is always deemed to be counfel

for

for the culprit, and surely every evidence in similar cases, is to tell, not what he thinks, which is less valid than what he hears, (as that may be true) but to say what he knows, and that only, as he is sworn to tell the truth, the whole truth, and nothing but the truth. Private opinion may be erroneous, if not false, and therefore, is liable to border on the reverse of truth, and how far that lies from the precincts of perjury, must be left to the publick.

Fifth Day. Colonel Sloper's evidence continued.

(P. 47. Lord George's trial) General Cholmondely says to this evidence,---you said you was present when Captain Winchingrode (one of Prince Ferdinand's Aids de Camp) Colonel Ligonier, and Colonel Fitzroy brought the orders. Now, I would ask you, whether the orders brought to Lord George Sackville by those gentlemen, were ever put in execution? To which Colonel Sloper answers,---Colonel Fitzroy's orders from the Prince, I have said I did not hear, Captain Winchingrode's and Captain (now Colonel) Ligonier's orders, were a quarter of an hour apart; I have said, that Captain Ligonier was a quarter of an hour with Lord George Sackville, and that the cavalry did not move till twenty ty minutes after Lord George left them with Colonel Fitzroy. The right of the cavalry I mean, so that in about three quarters of an hour after the first order, which was that of Captain Winchingrode's, the cavalry moved to the left, which is every thing I know of obedience, or tending to obedience of any orders I heard delivered. Upon which part of Colonel Sloper's evidence, General Cholmondely remarks (omitted in the Judge Advocate's account) and says, this is no answer to *any* question. I desire the evidence may be read, to see what the orders were.

(Evidence read)

OBSERVATION.

Indeed, Colonel Sloper's evidence is thro' the whole, dry and unsatisfactory, for his evidence consists of more that he does *not* know, than of any thing he *does*. The delays, the halts, and his own opinion thereon, being the sum total of his evidence; he indeed heard the orders given by Winchingrode, and Colonel Ligonier, and confirms them, this is the most material part; and for all the rest, the questions as well as answers relative to this witness seem to be superfluous and nugatory, as they produce no information, and as Lord George very justly observes, tend only to declamation.

(Page 50 Lord George's trial omitted in the Judge Advocate's account) The Prefident objects, and with reafon, againft Colonel Sloper's attempting to vindicate himfelf, who fays at the conclufion of his evidence, *I would juft fay a word upon what was mentioned yefterday by Lord George, he reflected upon me*, but was over-ruled, as he ought; fince nothing he could fay, could attone for fo cruel a profecution, not to fay defamation, of a perfon between life and death, and in the utmoft diftrefs.

(Page 51 Lord George's trial) Lord George objects againft the Pruffian Aid de Camp's evidence, as no way material, fince, though he intended, he delivered no orders, therefore it could make neither for, nor againft the prifoner, and would only take up the time of the court, but this was over-ruled. Derenthall gave in his evidence, which was nothing to the purpofe, and fo the Judge Advocate implies, faying (page 53.) It appears, that he was not prefent at any orders, which were fully known before, and it only, as the Judge Advocate fays, was admitted to fhew the impatience of the prince, which had no connection with proofs as to obedience or difobedience of orders, upon which (page ibid.) Lord George remarks, if you go into this fort of evidence, there will never be an end of the trial.

Obfervation

Observation on Colonel Pitt's Evidence.

As he was not present at any orders (p. 56. Lord George's trial) Lord George had received from Prince Ferdinand, he says he could not be a judge, how far any orders might, or might not have been executed, sooner by Lord George, from the time he might have received them; so that his whole evidence seems to be extorted from him, and at length to end only on distances, situation, marches, and halts, quite foreign to the point in question, viz. obedience or disobedience of orders, it is asked him, very unfairly we apprehend, whether the cavalry might not have marched quicker, and yet have been in a condition to do service, to which he answers, certainly much quicker, this is only private opinion, for it appears through the whole, that the horses were several times blown, which occasioned halts, this evidence also waves, very ingenuously, his answering to matters of opinion, though put to him repeatedly, (and page 57 Lord George's trial) he says, it seems to him matter of opinion, and should be glad to know, whether he was to answer it, upon which Lord Albemarle replies, it is an improper question; but it has been asked before; and yet it seems to have been asked by the only person in court, who was the best judge of its propriety, or impropriety. By this gentleman's evidence, it should seem that the Fir wood obstructed Lord George's keeping to the left, if he had so willed, as the horse under the marquis of Granby moved to the left by squadrons, in order to make room for the first line under Lord George to form, it was from this necessity we apprehend, and to form the more regularly, that Lord George, moved to the right, when his orders were to move to the left, which possibly, could not be at that instant obeyed. This is only a cursory remark on his then (perhaps necessary) variation from the orders, not intended to vindicate or accuse him; but it is equally left to the publick; but this evidence is supported (page 62. Lord George's trial) by that of the Marquis of Granby's, who tells the court, that Lord George said he only did it to form the line, and that when they came to the Fir-tree grove, there was any order to march to the left, in order to make room for two regiments that were in the first line, which they said, had not room to come up and form with the rest of the line.

Sixth Day. Remark on the Marquis of Granby's Evidence.

(Page 73. Lord George's trial) The marquis being asked his opinion *(still matters of of opinion'*) whether he thought that if Lord George had not halted the cavalry at different times, as he (Lord Granby) was advancing with it, that he (Lord Granby) would have come up in time, and in *proper order* to charge the enemy before they retired, after he had passed the wood? answered, he supposes he should have been up with the foot, if he had advanced as fast as he could without *ruining the cavalry*, or *blowing the horses*, this seems plainly to imply, that it could not be done without ruining the cavalry, or blowing the horses. N. B. Colonel Pitt deposes, that they could have marched much quicker and for service. (page 57 Lord George's trial) If it could not be done without blowing the horses, imports, as we apprehend, that it could not be done effectually and for service,---this remark is also left to the publick.

Sixth Day. Remarks on the Defence of Lord George.

Through the whole process, the examination steers directly to a scrutiny into the consequence of the halts, motions and marches, their positions, and changes, not to an enquiry whether orders were obeyed or not obeyed, or indeed into the moral propriety of their being obeyed in any other manner than they were,

were; which examination, seems to bear somewhat hard upon so great a distress, as the delinquent on trial, must be supposed to be in. As to the previous articles of the hour at which the horses were saddled, tents struck, &c. they seem to have been unnecessarily brought in. The point then in view should never be quitted, viz that of the orders; and first Ligonier's order to advance with the Cavalry, this seems through the process of the evidence to be complied with, the after order of Fitzroy, to advance with the British Cavalry to the left, as evidently was not complied with, and as they varied in number only, not in destination, perplexity might naturally arise in the breast of any man, though the material difference lay only in the distinction of *which*, not *whither*, *what part*, not to *what place*. These are categories evident enough, but yet, it seems, a perplexity might arise, as to the collateral categories--how?----and why? *how*, to the left, without proper guides? why the British cavalry, rather than the cavalry? These might not all seem expedient to a man on the spot, at the head of the British cavalry, and whose reputation lay in the success; therefore such a man would naturally enquire some explication on the propriety of the manœvre, as two aid de camps at one and the same time

brought

brought orders which varied from each other, I say, he who was no stranger to the precipitate delivery of orders (in the hurry of operation) thro' the channel of aids de camp, and these orders differing, the second countermanding the first in one respect, might very reasonably pause to reflect, on that reflection might see an impropriety in the immediate execution of such orders, and thereupon go and desire a verbal explanation of them from the commander in chief. From the tenor of the evidence it has not been proved, but rather to the contrary, that the halts were unnecessary, or improper. Hurry, confusion, blowing the horses, or attacking irregularly might have to all intents and purposes been the destruction of the whole British cavalry, ended in a defeat, and entirely undone what was so bravely effected by the British infantry, without the assistance of the cavalry. The time taken up by Lord George's going to Prince Ferdinand, did not affect the march of the cavalry, so far as to defeat the intentions of Prince Ferdinand, who perhaps was late in the dispatch of his orders, and would probably have altered the disposition of the manoeuvre in the same manner, as Lord George did, was he in the same situation. This is not alledged in Lord George's favour, but what

seems

seems to flow from the current of the evidence. There are several contradictions thro' the whole evidence in point of time, and distance (page 90. Lord George's Defence in Lord George's trial) Captain *Ligonier* says, that the enemy retired about three quarters of an hour, after he carried his orders, Colonel Fitzroy, on the other hand, says that the action lasted an hour and a half after his return to the Prince, which return, was by the evidence subsequent to *Ligonier*'s order. As to the distances, they also vary, and materially so, through the whole tenor of the evidence. Derenthall says, that he was present during the whole action with the attack of the infantry (p. 52. Lord George's trial) Winchingrode, that the infantry was engaged with the enemy; (p 11. ditto) and Fitzroy, that the Prince was only advancing (page 24. ibid) Sloper and Smith flatly contradict each other ---as to opinion (page 38 ibid) His opinion was, that Lord George was alarmed to a very great degree, &c. and Smith (page 105. ibid) believes that Lord George would have gone to face death that day had it been requisite, and denies, that his looks, manner, or behaviour, was different during the whole time, from what it was at any other. This evidence of Smith's, as to this particular, is supported by Captain

tain Hugo (p. 141. ibid) who swears, he saw nothing different in his looks, manner, or behaviour, different from any other time; Colonel Hotham deposes to the same purpose, but with more strength.

(Page 211, Judge Advocate's Proceedings) The Judge Advocate wishes that the period of time relative to Ligonier's and Fitzroy's orders, sworn to by different persons, had been the only contradiction in the evidence upon the trial, this implies that there had been more than one. The Judge Advocate has taken abundance of pains, (page 206 Judge Advocate's proceedings) to validate Colonel Sloper's testimony, which Lord George had endeavoured to discredit, and this he has done with a great deal of address and perspicuity, but has omitted saying any thing to his delivering opinion instead of matter of fact, or ascertaining consequences from his private judgment, instead of speaking to facts, things, and realities; much less has he attempted to support him in relating private conversations, reflections, and observations on Lord George's looks, which as we humbly apprehend should have been thought foreign to the dignity of that Court, over which in matters of law, he seemed to preside.

One of the main articles brought to invalidate the testimony of Colonel Sloper, by Lord George's evidence, is that he deposed

posed that Lord George was on the right of Bland's, when Captain Ligonier delivered his orders to him, whereas Lord George affirms that he was not at the head of Bland's at that time, and therefore could not have overheard the orders,---but on the contrary, he (Lord George) affirms to have been some where about the right of the Inniskilling's, but from the whole of the testimony, it appears that Colonel Sloper, was in the right. (page 210, Judge Advocate's account) The Judge Advocate agrees with Lord George, as he must with all the World, that it is inconclusive and improper to argue from the consequences, which the Cavalry's marching immediately would have had, and gives solid reasons for what he alledges.

In the whole, the arguments of the Judge Advocate are refined and admirably contrived, as Lord George's defence is strong, solid, and nervous, clear and perspicuous.

The evidence also through the whole seems to be as near truth, as the matter will admit of, though contradictory in several small particulars, such as the precision of time, place, and distance. As to the examination by the Judge Advocate, President, and others, we apprehend it led through the whole more to an enquiry into the consequences, which were merely accidental, and not so much as it should have
done

done, into the merits or demerits of Lord George, in point of obedience, or disobedience of orders, which, however, if we are at liberty, we should give softer terms, and call it *non-compliance* with orders, because it seems, that the orders were partly *obeyed*, though not instantly, and in every respect complied with though late, but at the same time cannot but believe, otherwise than that both judges and evidence acted and spoke from the dictates of honour and conscience, how much so ever they may have been swayed by natural tendancies, to which all Men are liable.

F I N I S.

CPSIA information can be obtained at www.ICGtesting.com
Printed in the USA
LVOW03s1842070814

398030LV00008B/361/P

9 781275 498891